The Stones Keep Watch

The Stones Keep Watch

Poems by

John Whitney Steele

© 2021 John Whitney Steele. All rights reserved.
This material may not be reproduced in any form, published,
reprinted, recorded, performed, broadcast,
rewritten or redistributed without
the explicit permission of John Whitney Steele.
All such actions are strictly prohibited by law.

Cover design by Shay Culligan
Cover art by John Whitney Steele

ISBN: 978-1-954353-97-8

Kelsay Books
502 South 1040 East, A-119
American Fork, Utah 84003
Kelsaybooks.com

for Thiya

Acknowledgments

I would like to thank the editors of the following publications, where versions of these poems have appeared, sometimes under different titles:

Blue Unicorn: "Big Bluestem"
Boulder Weekly: "Great Blue Heron" "Red Tail"
Chained Muse: "A Flash of Gold"
The Colorado Sun: "Lockdown"
Copperfield Review: "War Elephant"
Eastern Structures: "Listen"
Ekphrastic Review: "War Elephant"
The Literary Nest: "Deer Tracks," "The Buddha Said"
New Lyre: "Safe at Home"
Sparks of Calliope: "Posterity"

I would also like to give my appreciation to the Soul-Making Keats Literary Competition for awarding second prize to "A Flash of Gold."

The epigraph for this book is from Gail Tremblay's poem, "Indian Singing in 20th Century America," *Norton Anthology of Native Nations Poetry,* edited by Joy Harjo (2020).

"Light From Stars That Died" is based on Anne Herbert's essay, "Handy Tips on How to Behave at the Death of the World," first published in *Whole Earth Review,* 1995, p. 88, and reprinted in *The Sun Magazine,* March 2019. The italicized words are direct quotes from Herbert's essay.

Cover image: authors's photo of Hawk Tower, built by Robinson Jeffers for his wife, Una, Carmel, California.

Many thanks to my mentors in the MFA program at Western Colorado University: David Rothman, Ernie Hilbert, Julie Kane and Tyson Hausdoerffer. And a shout out to my poet friends, Gail ben Ezra, Dee Casalaina, Joslyn Green, Uche Ogbuji, Jere Paulmeno, Malinda Miller, Dale Schellenger, Susan Spear, Rich Uhrlaub, and Connie Zumpf, whose kind support and insightful comments proved indispensable in bringing this manuscript to fruition.

Contents

Listen	13
Grinnell Glacier	14
Light from Stars That Died	15
Whispers	17
Great Blue Heron	18
War Elephant	19
Red Tail	21
The Buddha Said	22
What's Required	24
Lockdown	28
Safe at Home	29
Posterity	30
Deer Tracks	31
Big Bluestem	33
A Flash of Gold	34
That Thou Art	35

*Even the stones sing
although their songs are infinitely
slower than the ones we learn
from trees. No human voice lasts
long enough to make such music sound.*
—Gail Tremblay

Listen

Listen to the river-rock percussion tones. Who hears
the water-dervish swirling over stones? Who hears?

Tibetan prayer flags slap a fence pole,
soprano through the malleus bones. Who hears?

Kids on skateboards grind across a bridge.
A mallard quacks to her young clones. Who hears?

A van with studded snow-tires thunders past,
pounding rap through residential zones. Who hears?

When Rumi cries out, *Shams*—angels faint.
The far-flung void intones, *Who hears?*

The one who turns when someone calls out, *John*—
feels the question stirring in his bones, *Who hears?*

Grinnell Glacier

The glacier glistens as it glides downslope.
Kneeling, knowing nothing lives forever,
ear to the earth, earnest in prayer,
I listen to the drip, drip, drip,
the silent sorrow of silver ice.
Softly, now, I pronounce your name,
Grinnell Glacier. You glimmer, then glare.
Melting slowly, you slide downslope.
Sorry to say, it's too late to save you.
But you'll leave a lasting legacy in stone:
the cirque, the saddle, the sand, the gravel,
the tumult of talus before the terminal moraine.
Many will come to marvel at your monuments.
But when the drip, drip, drip, of your melting
stops, and your streams stop, along with the cascades
crashing through crevices and over the cliff,
and your emerald lake is forever empty,
we'll wonder what we were thinking and why
we allowed the waters of the world to overwhelm her shores.

Light from Stars That Died

—after Anne Herbert

It seeps in like a dream: melting ice,
rising tides, rainforests on the wane,

ever more surreal extremes,
and then you know it in your bones—

It's over.

How then shall we live?

It's probably okay to speak the truth,
terminal patients have a right to know.

Might as well avoid harmful activities
when doing the last things done by humans.

Don't forget your debt to ancestors
all the way back through fish to protozoans.

Contemplate the light from stars that died
billions of years before our sun was born.

Consider all you've been through in your life,
where you came from, how long it took to make

you what you are: conscious flesh. Forgive
yourself for failing. You are only human.

Write thank-you notes—apologize to Earth.
Love all that lives before the screen goes dark.

The stones keep watch, along with trees, and stars,
and haggard people fingering their phones.

If you love them let them know.

Whispers

Whispers in my ear, half-heard, ethereal,
call forth memories that fade before they're known,
a frightened child, prowling wolves, confused familiars,
so familiar I mistake them for my own.

Lucid dreams come and go like late spring snow.
I run along behind and try to catch the light
that falls like dust from angel's feet. I'm far too slow.
I stop to catch my breath, and though I search all night,

I cannot find one particle of heaven's light,
nor can I recreate it from the alpenglow.
And so I run my fingers through the dust, uncover
clues that lead me to a grove where bird-wings flutter.
I sit all night and listen till I come to know
I am drenched in light from head to toe.

Great Blue Heron

Walking around the lake this afternoon,
something about the cottonwood leaves, strewn
along the shore, and how the colors glowed,
and the reflections in the water slowed
me down, let me begin to see, if you
know what I mean, as if I were seeing through
God's eyes, or dog eyes. Who knows what dogs see,
or how they manage to project such glee,
such wag-tailed joy, despite the constant strain
of living within range of wretched brains.
The sixth extinction can't be turned around.
If nothing's done, and soon, we too will drown,
weighed down by overgrown prefrontal lobes,
plotting and scheming, sending out space-probes
beyond the reach of our sun's golden light,
in hopeless hope of finding other life,
a garden paradise, not yet sucked dry—
Pulled back to planet earth, the sudden cries
of geese, waddling away, dogs in chase,
geese, water-born, gliding along, dogs racing
to catch up. Suddenly, across the lake,
that prehistoric great blue heron takes
flight, cries out, in its ancient, haunting voice,
asking, asking: *Do we have a choice?*

War Elephant

—after a painting from the Akbarnama: "Akbar inspecting a wild elephant captured from a herd near Malwa in 1564."

Hind legs bound and tied to tree, you stand
poised, ears back, trunk coiled. Captive,
yet you stand with such fierce dignity,
stamping the earth with your tremendous foot.
You tower high above the emperor,
seated there upon his prancing horse,
spear held aloft, as if to fend you off.
A horde of captors stands by holding spears.
How dare they do this to you, noble beast?
You gaze at them with such deep, steady eyes.
Do they not know you mean no harm?
Two other elephants walk by, subdued,
content to let mahouts ride on their backs.

Descendant of the ten-tusked Airavata,
who sucks up water from the underworld,
sprays it into clouds, and rides upon
the skies with Thunderous-Indra on his back,
you will lead the charge of Akbar's troops
with iron-spiked tusks, ears splayed wide,
whip-like trunk adorned with chains and balls.

How many of your kind died crossing the Alps
with Hannibal? When he got you drunk
and whipped you to a frenzy, remember those
iron-clad Roman soldiers, how they fled?

When you face extinction at the hands
of those you died for, will you not fight back?
Why not call on Lightning-Wielding Indra
to descend on Ten-Tusked Airavata's back,
thunderbolt the poachers' helicopters
and bring them crashing blood-stained to the ground?

Red Tail

His yellow talons clutch a gnarled branch
not ten yards away. His regal head
turns to take me in. When he turns back
to look across the lake, I take one step

toward him, another. He lifts and swivels his head,
tilts it down, drills his laser eyes
through my tail-tucked chihuahua. I pull her
back behind me, whisper, *Maya, stay.*

He plumps his creampuff chest, turns away,
pivots forward, spreads his wings, lifts
his red-fanned tail, excretes a stream of white.

I scoop up Maya, hold her tight,
look into her almond-sunshine eyes.

The hawk's dark gaze turns back toward his prey.

The Buddha Said

The world's on fire.

Fueled by fear,
us versus them,

Frantic cycles
of grasping, hatred,

fight, flight, freeze.

The Buddha said,
The world's on fire.

How much more so

now.

    And yet

we still deny it.

What more does it take?

The threat
of nuclear war,

the paralyzed panic
of icecap meltdown,

the ravages of Covid,
people of color squelched,

lynchings, protests,
tear gas, riots.

The world's on fire

now.

        And yet

we still deny it.

There's no time
for blame and shame.

Put aside
your monkey-mind.

Dowse the flames
that rage within you.

The world's on fire.
Both your hands are free.

What's Required

I

Bursting in, she screams, *Killer bees,*
help! I grab a magazine,
Thwack, thwack. Kill four, just like that.
Find more buzzing around a crack,
the entrance to their home
underneath a flagstone,
the steppingstone to our backdoor.
Inside, four wasps, dead on the floor.

My thoughts swarm: killing in self-defense—
am I hardwired for that? Killing born
of hatred is an aberration.
Turn the other cheek?—Uncommon sense—
am I hardwired for that, or torn
between the two, seeking salvation?

II

Torn between the two, seeking salvation,
watching, waiting, fearing this nation
divided, roiled by a would-be tyrant.
Are we not hardwired to bring down a tyrant?
Democracy's a high-wire act.
We must distinguish fiction, fact.
Rumors, conspiracies, spread like wildfire.
Can I shake off inertia, do what's required?

I won't pretend assassination never crossed my mind.
But I'm no Brutus. And Caesar's blood
failed to save the nation.
I pay attention, bide my time,
consider Gandhi's labor of love,
his steadfast dedication.

III

Consider Gandhi's dedication,
how his fasts and protests swept the nation,
his boycotts, marches, forced out Britain,
his beloved India split,
and Hindu-Muslim bloodbaths broke
his heart. How he never cast off the yoke,
how he faced death with aplomb:
shot in the gut, gasping, *Hey Ram!*

I'm not cut out to be a martyr.
*I just let my animal body love
what it loves.* I'm not one to roar
like a lion against state-sanctioned murders.
I'd rather sit and coo with the doves.
But democracy's something worth fighting for.

IV

Democracy's something worth fighting for.
Not me alone against the whole world.
I'd stand on the shoulders of King and Parks

and so many others, bending the arc.
Follow their example, not cling to results,
never be swayed by praise or insults,
rein in anger, steer clear of hatred,
find my own way, make it sacred.

But I need to start in my own backyard—
those damned wasps.
They won't let us near our garden shed.
My wife's body, swollen and scarred,
leaves me no choice. The wasps
must be dealt with—tonight before bed.

V

The wasps must be dealt with—tonight, before bed.
We need to get into our garden shed.
My wife's been stung and traumatized.
Everything she says is dramatized.
What choice do I have but get out the hose,
put on an extra layer of clothes,
and flood their home, hoping they drown
in their sleep feeling safe and sound.

Hoping they drowned, feeling safe and sound,
I get up close and look for signs of life.
All is quiet, nothing moves. My relief
is bittersweet. Did I just drown
an entire community? I tell my wife,
I think it worked. We'll have to wait and see.

VI

I thought I'd done them in. This morning I see
how wrong I was. It wasn't meant to be.
My wife's already found an exterminator,
stuck the number on the refrigerator.
It's up to me to make the call,
engage a pro to kill the whole cabal.
The hired assassin makes it look so easy,
but killing sentient beings makes me queasy.

I open the shed, get out the lawn mower.
The simple work of mowing calms my mind.
I trim around the edges, rake the leaves,
dump them in the compost. One more chore
out of the way. Now I can unwind.
My voter phone-bank calls will be a breeze.

Lockdown

Yesterday, snowed-in felt almost normal.

Today, as trees loaded with snow awake
to cold blue skies, the world is all aglow.

How could any virus survive such beauty?

By the lake, I keep my six-foot distance,
but what could be more intimate than snow

cascading from a tree onto my brow?

Safe at Home

> *My life is not this steeply sloping hour,*
> *in which you see me hurrying.*
>   —Rainer Maria Rilke, tr. Robert Bly

Home alone, far from the sloping hour,
life is not as hectic as before.
Solitude is neither sweet nor sour.

As a bee bores down into a flower,
I contemplate the adage: less is more.
Home alone, far from the sloping hour,

though not immune from sickness, death, or sorrow,
I won't let fear control me anymore.
My solitude is neither sweet nor sour.

I think of Jeffers building Una's tower.
When visitors come knocking at the door
to find him hard at work, at any hour,

does he crack a smile or does he scowl,
or just keep hauling stone up from the shore,
his solitude, neither sweet nor sour?

Our situation's dire. We must change now or—
follow close behind the dinosaur.
Yet I feel safe, far from the sloping hour,
This solitude is neither sweet nor sour.

Posterity

She placed her palm on torchlit stone,
spit red ochre at her hand,
left her mark, her stenciled clone,
a work of art, Neanderthal,
a language we still understand.

The permafrost is melting now,
releasing long held secrets:
fifty-thousand-year-old wolf pups
perfectly preserved, reindeer
killed by anthrax, disinterred.

When human beings are no more
what will we have left behind?
What hope have I to leave a mark
some future race will find?

Deer Tracks

I've beaten my own path
through meadows that in spring

revealed mere hints of trails
left by wintering deer.

Trained by daily walks
that tramp down traceless deer-paths

my slipshod mind
starts to fall in line.

But I prefer to wander
along untrammeled forks

that meander into nothing—
as if the deer had disappeared

mid-step, or a wind-borne thought
had faded into the fog of no one there…

until a trickle in the stream-bed
from last night's rain, the crunch

of a pinecone underfoot,
percolates through my brain,

and like a newborn waking
from a dreamless sleep,

I look around, wide-eyed.
Enthralled by the flight of a hawk,

I recall those child-long days
spent gazing through God's eye.

Back then, when I scaled cliffs,
looked down, knowing I could fall,

I was sure that something in me
would not, could not die—

The hawk's no longer visible.
What do hawks make of this world?

Eyebrow to eyebrow with Death,
do they too, smell his breath?

Big Bluestem

Your turkey-footed seed-heads brush my shoulders.
As I reach out to touch your yellowed leaves
I think of your deep roots, how they hold

the earth in place. I can almost see
your wind-tossed wands slow-dancing all the way
from the Rockies to the Mississippi,

as they once did. But now, with climate change
and overgrazing driving your decline,
mere patches of your former range remain.

Who knows how much longer you'll survive,
how long the wind will sing your tall grass blues?
Do you know what it means to be alive?

The child in me wants to believe you do.
When the last of your kind wilts away,
who will greet the morning laced with dew?

A Flash of Gold

A flash of gold descends onto a blade
of grass, resolves into a dragonfly,
lingers there, airing its wings as I

creep in close, hold my breath, evade
its wary glance. Moments like this—where every
second counts—it's what I live for.

Binoculars in focus, I gaze into its eye,
a speck of golden reverie,
lose myself in its translucent body.

The thought of reaching for my phone
breaks my dragonfly samadhi.
Before I notice, it has flown.

I can't stop looking, listening, for the drone
of see-through wings, the lightning flash of gold.

That Thou Art

'Tat tvam asi' That thou art—Chandogya Upanishad 6.8.7

        The Word   That
        made flesh   thou

thou tree-descended human   limbs intertwined
    with stars   neither this nor that   not this

not that   the fox squirrel on the eave lapping snowmelt
    teeth clacking on a rock hard-seed   neither this

    nor that   the seed from the most ancient tree
whose roots stretch far beyond the fungal filaments

tap quarks   black holes   dark matter   out beyond
talk of God   luminous emptiness   birth and death

    the scaffolding you need and don't
need for survival   things you think you know

    things you don't know   matter
    eye ear nose tongue

    That

About the Author

John Whitney Steele is a psychologist, yoga teacher, assistant editor of *Think: A Journal of Poetry, Fiction and Essays,* and graduate of the MFA Poetry Program at Western Colorado University, where he studied with Julie Kane, David Rothman, and Ernest Hilbert. A Pushcart Prize nominee, his poetry and book reviews have appeared in numerous print and online journals. Born in Toronto and raised among the pines and silver birches of Foot's Bay, Ontario, John lives in Boulder, Colorado where he often encounters his muse wandering in the mountains.

John can be found at
johnwhitneysteelepoet.com.

www.ingramcontent.com/pod-product-compliance
Lightning Source LLC
Chambersburg PA
CBHW021029090426
42738CB00007B/949